Finding Things

John Malam

Contents

OXFORD

UNIVERSITY PRESS

Introduction

Have you ever been on a hunt for something? Have you ever found something that was hidden? It's very exciting to find things!

These children are at the seaside. What will they find?

Crab

Shells

All the things in this book were hidden.
Then someone found them!
Here are just two of the hidden
things you will find out about.

- An animal from long ago.
  Where was it found?

You can find it on page 4

Seaweed

- A boy who was a king.
  What was his name?

You can find him on page 10

Fish

Fossil finder

My name is
Sue Hendrickson.
It's my job to look
for **fossils**. One day
I was looking for
fossils in the side
of a hill. I found a little bit of old
bone. Then I saw lots more bones.
I had found a **dinosaur**!

USA

Faith, South Dakota

This is where Sue found the dinosaur.

A team of people dug the bones out. They joined them up to make a **skeleton**. The bones were from a *Tyrannosaurus Rex*. Some of its teeth were 30 cm long! The dinosaur I found is now called Sue, after me.

A *Tyrannosaurus Rex* skeleton in a museum.

Buried treasure

This is the true story of a farmer from the UK. His name is Eric Lawes. One day he was looking for a hammer in a field. He was using a metal detector to look for it.

This is where Eric found the treasure.

UK

Hoxne, Suffolk

Metal detectors are used to find hidden metal.

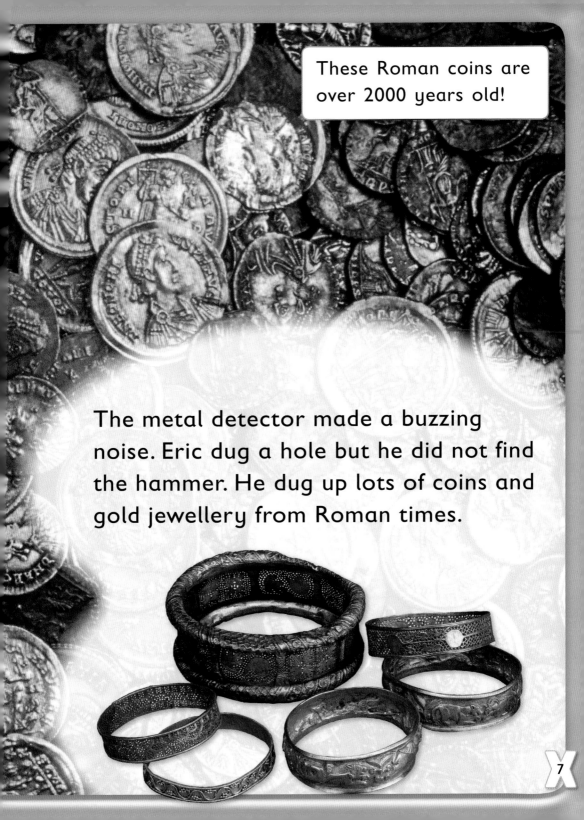

These Roman coins are over 2000 years old!

The metal detector made a buzzing noise. Eric dug a hole but he did not find the hammer. He dug up lots of coins and gold jewellery from Roman times.

Colossal squid

Can you find?

Colossal squid are shy animals. They live at the bottom of the deep, dark sea. They live so deep that they are very hard to find.

In the past, sailors told stories about sea **monsters**. We now know that these monsters were colossal squid.

Stories tell of monsters attacking ships.

In 2007, a colossal squid was pulled up on a fishing line. The men who found it got a big surprise!

It was the biggest squid ever found!

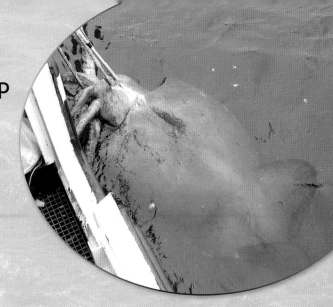

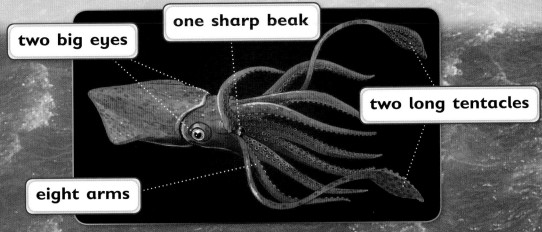

two big eyes

one sharp beak

two long tentacles

eight arms

The world's biggest squid

When was it found?	2007
Where was it found?	Ross Sea, Antarctica
How long was it?	14 m
How heavy was it?	495 kg
Who found it?	Fishermen from New Zealand
Where is it now?	In the Museum of New Zealand

Boy-king of Egypt

Can you find?

A long, long time ago, a 9-year-old boy became a king. He was the king of Egypt. He was very rich. His name was *Tutankhamen*. You say his name like this: "too–tan–car–men".

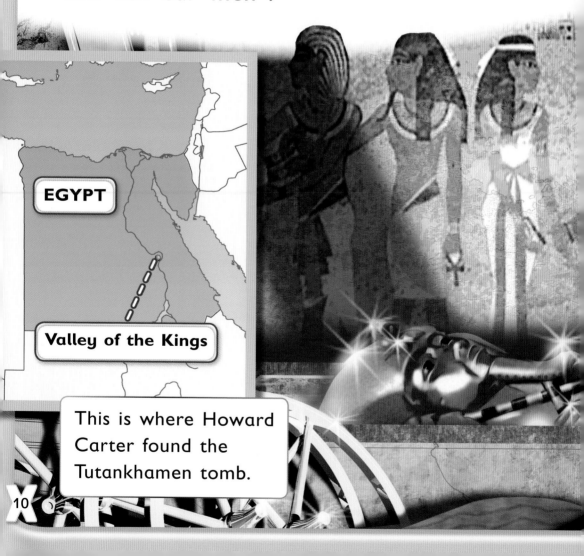

EGYPT

Valley of the Kings

This is where Howard Carter found the Tutankhamen tomb.

After he died, he was buried with all his treasure. Thousands of years later, his **tomb** was found. It was found by Howard Carter. Carter peeped inside and said he could see "wonderful things".

Tutankhamen's gold face mask

The tomb was full of riches.

Long-lost liner

Can you find?

In 1912, the biggest ship in the world was called *Titanic*. The ship's builders thought it would never sink. Here is the story of how *Titanic* did sink!

Wednesday, 10 April, 1912

① The *Titanic* set sail from Southampton. She started to cross the Atlantic Ocean to America.

Sunday, 14 April, 1912

② Just before midnight, *Titanic* hit an **iceberg**! It made a big hole in the bottom of the ship.

Monday, 15 April, 1912

❸ Early the next morning, *Titanic* sank. About 1500 people drowned.

Thursday, 18 April, 1912

❹ Some lucky people were rescued by a ship called *Carpathia*. They reached dry land.

Sunday, 1 September, 1985

❺ The *Titanic* shipwreck was found by a team of underwater explorers.

Out of this world

Can you find?

What about finding things in space?
Scientists use big **telescopes** to look into
space. Sometimes they find new things. In
1930, Clyde Tombaugh looked through
a big telescope. He found a tiny planet,
far away from Earth. The planet was
given the name *Pluto*.

A rocket leaving Earth
to explore space.

A spacecraft on the surface of Mars.

Scientists send **spacecraft** to explore the planets. The spacecraft send pictures of the planets back to Earth. Some planets are far away. It took 20 years for a spacecraft to reach Pluto!

Pluto

FACT

In 2006, scientists decided that Pluto was too small to be a planet. Today, it is called a 'minor' or 'dwarf' planet.

Glossary

dinosaur	a huge lizard that lived millions of years ago
fossil	part of a dead plant or animal that has become hard like a rock
iceberg	a very big piece of ice in the sea
monster	a large, frightening animal in stories
skeleton	all the bones inside the body of a person or an animal
spacecraft	a vehicle that can travel in space
telescope	a tube people look through to see things that are far away
tomb	a place where a dead person's body is buried

Index